*Spotlight
Poets*

Here in My Mind

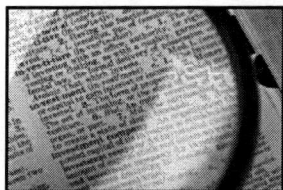

Edited by Heather Killingray & Steph Park-Pirie

Spotlight Poets

First published in Great Britain in 2005 by
SPOTLIGHT POETS
Remus House
Coltsfoot Drive
Peterborough
PE2 9JX
Telephone: 01733 898102
Fax: 01733 313524
Website: www.forwardpress.co.uk

SB ISBN 1 84077 131 3

Foreword

As a nation of poetry writers and lovers, many of us are still surprisingly reluctant to go out and actually buy the books we cherish so much. Often when searching out the work of newer and less known authors it becomes a near impossible mission to track down the sort of books you require. In an effort to break away from the endless clutter of seemingly unrelated poems from authors we know nothing or little about; Spotlight Poets has opened up a doorway to something quite special.

Here in My Mind is a collection of poems to be cherished forever; featuring the work of eleven captivating poets each with a selection of their very best work. Placing that alongside their own personal profile gives a complete feel for the way each author works, allowing for a clearer idea of the true feelings and reasoning behind the poems.

The poems and poets have been chosen and presented in a complementary anthology that offers a variety of ideals and ideas, capable of moving the heart, mind and soul of the reader.

Heather Killingray & Steph Park-Pirie

Contents

The Authors
& Poems

Liz Osmond

My name is Liz and I have been in two shared anthologies before. I still submit regularly and write often.

Last year had been quite hard. Surgery in January and other people being ill. But out there in the garden's tranquillity I've recharged my batteries! Nature is a great healer.

Thanks and love to all the friends who helped out, Julie, Joan, Glen, Angela. To my friends who I see often, Brenda and her Irish setters, George, Barney, Ella and Poppy! To my parents who struggle on to retain their fierce pride and independence.

My poetry is not 'fancy stuff', just from the heart and of life.

I enjoy writing and hope some of my worlds will strike a chord in the heart of a reader.

Silhouettes

On the patio at 11pm
Bats gliding,
Diving after moths
Stars emerging
Jewels of the night.
The trees silhouetted
Against the darkening sky.
Night changes.
Our world sleeps
But theirs awakens.
The chill is there
But it's good out here.
Listen, and you may hear
A squeak from the bats
A snort from a passing hedgehog.
Something tells me, I'll never be wealthy
But who cares?
You can fret too much about
What you haven't got
And completely miss what you have.
    - Life -
I am so glad I can look and
See a worm, a lizard
Or a bird in the tree
Things we need no money for
The Lord created free!

The Escape Artists

(My friend's Irish setters are quite adept at breaking out and leading us a merry dance)

We need no tunnels
We just jump over
Away to the fields
The mud and the water
Smell that rabbit
Startle a bird
All the while worried voices
We can hear!
Oh all this fun, Barney soaking wet
George on the run.
Finally back they come
Delivered by kind souls
Into caring hands.
Noses in their water
Red coats not fit for the show ring!
Oh relief!
Safe back home
Me to a cuppa
Them to their bones!

Red Shadow

(Red Shadow is Ella, an Irish setter!)

I turn and you are there.
So unconditionally you give your love
Do you know love?
What is it to you?

You beautiful creature
Never having known cruelty
Only loving hands.
I look deep into your almond eyes.

Do you know just a little
Of this human mind?
Soft hands on soft coat
Lovely red shadow, the doggy kind!

Gentle eyes, look deep into mine
I'm sure you can read my mind!
Or are you thinking
I've got a soft one here, I'll wrap her
Round my left paw . . . ?

Angel In The Kitchen

(In my friend's kitchen her Irish setter kept looking transfixed at a corner and we were both convinced an angel was visiting)

Where are you
We cannot see you
But you're welcome
Come to stay!

Our friend can see you
She looks askance
Inquisitive eyes
Where are you, if only for her eyes . . . ?

For Julie

My friend in your radio shack
Computers, wires,
Radio crackling
As you talk to the boys
Across 'the pond'
Always busy designing
Something new
The tower in the garden
With its aerials on.
The turtle doves perch
Upon them
And sometimes the owl
You're in your element
Buried in your shack.
I don't understand it at all!
Too technical by far
So I stick to the garden
And talk to the neighbour
Over the fence!
So much easier by far!

In Praise Of Joan

My dear friend
Makes wonderful lasagne!
She got up to tend me
When I was ill!

More than a mum to me
This woman's worth
A million.

In eight years of friendship,
We have shared many things,
Illness and joys.

Thank you for inviting me
Into your home
Thank you for your friendship
So much more this woman's worth!

Just Dreams

I wish I were a whale
Swimming free with friends,
Or just borne into the
Watery depths by a mother
Who will love me for years
Who will gently carry me to the surface air
To fill my lungs, and bear me on her back when I tire.

As we swim the oceans together,
She will teach me many things.
The only thing I have to fear, ironically, is man.
Some other being who is intelligent such as I
Yet destroys us and his own kind . . .

We dive to great depths,
Mankind, he sees the stars!
His own planet he knows not . . .
Yet he aspires to land on Mars!

Or do I wish to be a kestrel
Soaring to the heights?
Looking down on human ants
And wondering at their daily rants!

A dreamer, I believe in unicorns
And Pegasus, and loving Mother's arms!
Perhaps I just have to find it in my heart to believe
In the things I've never had . . .
The ultimate is love . . .

Pictures In The Fire . . .

Autumn bonfire
Crackling away
As I burn up the leaves of yesterday . . .
Throw in the hurts, the pain, the fear.
Grief that assailed me throughout the year . . .
Stand with hot tea
Looking at flames,
Mind wanders back to sunny days.
I stand alone,
The flames are licking,
I take your photos
And throw them in . . .
Not a baptism of fire,
More a funeral pyre.
The celluloid shrivels up and hisses.
I look and wonder,
But not too much!
Just like throwing on spent leaves
On this crisp autumn morning,
I've just cleared you out of my closet . . .
No more mourning . . .

Do Birds Get Scared

Of heights . . . ?
I see them gently stretching their new-found wings
As they pop out of the nest box
Each late spring.

I think of my own fear of heights,
And look at these tiny things,
Up a big tree, being yelled at by Mum!
Plop, one falls . . .

Luckily, I get to him before the cat,
His tiny heart beating so fast.
Out comes the ladder,
And the tiny bird goes back to safety . . .

Mum comes down and feeds him,
They fly away! Me, I'm suddenly scared!
I'm stuck up this ladder,
Help! I need a bird!

My Dog

(Written years ago)

Has a silky coat
And knowing eyes.
He sits beside me
Expecting nothing,
But hoping for kind words
And a square meal . . .
If he's lucky
To stretch out on my bed.
If only humans
Were more like doggy kind.
The love they give is unquestioning
And gives great peace of mind . . .
Humans!
Well, they just get in the way
And haven't a tail to wag
So we don't know if
They're happy or sad!

Foot Fetish

My friend's dog
Loves feet . . .
Clean or mucky
She's not fussy!
Ticklish?
Don't let her near
To lick between
Your toes!
Funny dog also likes
Being hoovered
Or should we say
Dysoned?
For fear of being sued!
So I Dyson her
And she licks my toes!
What a funny pair we are.

Wagging Tails

The best welcome on a cloudy day
A wagging tail or four!
How can you compare the trust
That is there?

Completely reliant on you
For praise, for food, for everything good
Repaid in full so many times
With the only way they know . . .

Wagging tails!

Memorial Rose Garden, (Beth Shalom)

(Beth Shalom is the Holocaust Center at Ollerton, Notts.
I would defy anyone to walk out of there without crying)

I smelt the perfume of roses
When I left that awful place
That taught me so many things
Perhaps I had been dreading
But didn't really want to know.
Like a close-up in photography
Which shows up all the faults!
I wept and wondered
What those people smelt,
Or saw,
Or felt.
What was their lot . . .
When no one came in all
Those years to liberate them?
They had nothing . . .
Not even scent of roses to cling to.

Just smoke pyres
In their place.

From A Dreamer Who Cannot Sleep!

So here I am again,
The dreamer who cannot sleep!
Bit of a contradiction
That's me!
Just an enigma . . .
An Earth sign who loves water,
So nothing rhymes just now,
It's black outside,
And the owl calls from his tree.
It's not a hunter's moon.
No wolves cry,
No Indians brave,
To share the ancient wisdom
The shaman who see spirits in the fire
And can heal every ill with forest law.

So the Mayans went!
The crystal skull was found.
More mysteries abound.
Do the dolphins of the deep
Atlantis secrets keep?
I think they could talk if they chose,
But we are not ready to hear.
So, aliens we look for,
What if they landed?
Would we shoot them from the skies?
No answers on a postcard needed!
We look, we see, but do we understand . . . ?
A lovely world
But have the aliens already landed?

Daphne Elizabeth Kynaston

I am a 55-year-old retired RGN, married with two grown-up children, three grandsons and another one on the way. I live in Droylsden, Manchester.

My nursing career was prematurely cut short after a car accident in 1998 and I have been writing poetry since my retirement. I have been a Christian for 37 years, and my poetry is an expression of my faith in God.

Throughout my nursing career I have seen much suffering and distress brought about by sickness and death, but I have also seen what faith in God can do. It goes beyond the circumstance and changes the person.

I am very involved within the church, teaching, preaching, worship-leading, and directing missions, (amongst other things.) Poetry is a communication of what's going on inside, and I get my inspiration from my faith in God, the Bible and church life in general.

My poetry has been well received, I have written two poetic eulogies which were read out at funerals, but I also write light-hearted material with a message, or punchline at the end.

My poems are aimed at church groups and as such they are appropriate for people of all ages. They have been read in schools, youth groups and church services.

I try to impart the Christian ethos in a way that people can relate to. The poems talk about our strengths and weaknesses, and what the Bible teaches about them.

Last year I put together a poetry booklet which helped to raise funds for us to go to an orphanage in India and help them to put a roof on. These booklets sold quite well, and when we approached Wesley Owen (a big Christian bookshop in Manchester and Stockport) they said that if I produced another such booklet they would market it on a sale or return basis.

I just want my poems to bless people.

Although I'm Only Me

God, Your love is boundless,
And although I'm only me,
Your care for me is beautiful,
Much deeper than the sea,
And so I want to thank You,
For this love which came to me,
When You sent Your Son, Jesus,
To die on Calvary's tree.

I know I have done wrongly
So many many times
My guilt and sin deserved Your wrath,
Your sentence for my crimes,
But Jesus took my punishment,
And said I could go free,
'Cause God, to You I'm precious,
Although, I'm only me.

As Each Member Does Its Part

'As each member does its part - oh don't be daft,'
Said the finger to the scapular and laughed.
'I'm working every day without a penny for my pay
So I'm giving up the job this very day.'

'I don't blame him,' said the kidney to the toe,
'This work is full of misery and woe.
Cleaning blood every day without a penny for my pay
How can anyone expect me to stay?'

So the mutiny went on throughout the body
Instead of work many took themselves a hobby.
A few old faithfuls, they did stay, carried on from day to day
But the body did not function as it may.

Now the outcome of the strike was not so good
Because the body did not function as it should.
So discussions were begun on how the system should be run
But it was much too late, the deed was done.

Rigor mortis had set in I'm sure you'll know
Though the body looked so peaceful there on show.
All the signs of life were gone, the race had all been run
And the living of that life had all been done.

Now the moral of this tale, so well we know
Is that the body of Christ down here below
Consists of you and me being what we're meant to be
To keep the body working in perfect harmony.

Celebrate Life

Let's celebrate life, it's a wonderful thing,
A flower in bloom or a bird on the wing
Their beauty and song is the tribute they bring.
It's all God's creation in praise to their king.

Life comes so quickly and goes by so fast
And we're often astonished at all that has passed
But trusting in Jesus as humbly we pray
He gives us the grace to conquer each day.

God shines His light every step of the way
His Word is a lamp to my path day by day
The trials and testing so often in sight
Are nothing compared to His glorious light.

So we celebrate life, it's a wonderful thing
Treasures in Jesus, faith on the wing
And so on this new day our tribute we bring
To Jesus the Saviour and life-giving King.

God Holds The Key

Psychology, what a wonderful thing!
It's the study of human imagining.
Where do we run to when things do not rhyme,
And we no longer hear the bells of joy chime
When the song in our heart sounds out of tune,
And the end of the day can't come too soon
We don't see life's picture, it's just out of sight.
And the vision within is the darkness of night?

We could run here, or we could run there
But who understands our inner despair
And who holds the key to the problems of life,
The whys and the wherefores, the reason for strife
Who can we turn to when things go awry,
Who understands us, and who tells us why?
The psychiatrists say, 'It's all in your mind,
Just let us delve and you'll see it defined.'

But God is our maker, He formed every part,
And He knows the confines of every heart.
He is the answer, our search has ended,
Fullness of joy is what He intended.
The problems and strife are all born of sin,
But He took them all to give peace within.
His life and His Spirit to all He will give,
As we come to Him, He's so kind to forgive.

Search where we may we will not find peace
Till we look to Jesus who carried our grief.
Although we have sinned again and again,
He paid our ransom, took the suff'ring and pain.
He's not given me a spirit of fear
But of love and of power and a mind that is clear.
In Jesus our Lord we can be made free,
'Cause to all of life's problems, He holds the key.

Greatest In The Kingdom

What does my Pastor think of me?
I hope my position is what it should be
I'm greatest in the Kingdom you see.
I'm always there making the grade
Putting the others right into the shade
I hinder their progress, making them fall
But I'm always up, and walking tall.

I'll speak to my brother while shaking his hand
Looking over his shoulder, surveying the land
Must give the impression I love him a lot
While searching to see what the others have got
I'll be up to date, keep up with the plot.
What's everyone doing? Now what can I find?
Must keep my position and not lag behind.

Oh! There's Mrs Gossip, she is on top form
She's wearing down Phyllis who looks so forlorn
There's Mr Complainer still having a go
He tears into Harvey who's feeling so low
How nice to have people working for free
To bring down the others and elevate me
I'm the greatest in the Kingdom you see.

Now this is the way that the world finds position
By walking on people who get in the way
But now we must make an important decision
To follow God's teaching, through Jesus the Way
Let's prefer one another, pick me up when I fall
Complaining and gossip have no place at all
We must become humble to follow God's call.

For the least in the Kingdom is the greatest of all.

Lazarus

Now a message came to the Lord one day
Which said, 'Will You please come quickly,
He whom You love, in Bethany
Has become extremely sickly.'
But Jesus declared, 'He will not die,
Though the forces of death come very nigh,
And those all around will hear the story,
For this has happened to show forth God's glory.'

Now Jesus stayed where He was two days more,
Then He met up with Martha, and Mary He saw,
His friend had died, in the grave clothes he lay,
In that dark lonely tomb it was the fourth day.
Lazarus rotting? The thought was repelling,
By now the inside of the tomb would be smelling.
'If You had been here Lord, he would not have died.'
But the Lord said, 'Believe this, your brother will rise!'

They removed the stone from the mouth of the cave,
And Jesus said loudly, 'Come forth from the grave!'
Lazarus came out, the grave clothes still round him,
But Jesus said, 'Loose him from that which has bound him.'
Now Mary and Martha, in grief they had questioned,
But there was no doubt, Jesus brought resurrection.
And today He gives life to you and to me,
From the bondage of death, He's still setting men free.

Peace, Be Still

What does it matter if my skies are grey,
And the shadows of night come to darken my way.
If the harsh storms of life blow with all of their might
And I can't see my way, only darkness of night?

What does it matter if storm clouds are near,
And the elements try to bring torment and fear?
In Jesus, the faithful friend by my side
I have a constant companion and guide.

I walk by faith and not by sight,
By God's unquenchable guiding light
His Word is my lamp and by its broad beam
Things are quite different from what they may seem.

It shows me the way, the truth and the life,
And leads me through all the worry and strife.
I'd rather trust Jesus, He says, 'Peace, be still'
When I walk in His footsteps, and follow His will.

The Deceiver

We are warned in the Bible that lies and deceit
Will be brought in by Satan and laid at our feet.
As an angel of light he will come to deceive us,
Such fables and stories he'll craftily weave us.
Nothing ugly or vile because we won't receive it,
But close to the truth so the saints can believe it.
Now what is more crafty than truth that's been twisted
Nothing blatantly nasty, but an image that's misted?

He comes to our church and sits down beside us,
Innuendoes and lies he spins to deride us.
'Have faith in God', he knows that will please us,
But he fails to confide that it's only 'in Jesus'.
Of course he knows we need a belief,
But, 'Don't be too committed, it will only bring grief.'
He tells us we have to be holy and true,
But, 'Don't be so eager, tomorrow will do.'

Now these days he's got most folk in a spin,
And they don't know the depth of the trouble they're in.
They look over here and they look over there,
But they don't find the answers to ease their despair.
We only find truth as we look in God's Word,
So don't you believe all the lies you have heard.
The signposts are pointing, so plainly they say,
Jesus Christ is the truth, the life and the way.

The Good Shepherd

Our God is a good God, I know His love divine
His hand of mercy and of grace is with me all the time.
Although I'm prone to wander from pastures so sublime,
He gently leads me back again and tells me, 'You are Mine.'

Forever the 'Good Shepherd' I know His love always,
He leads me into pastures green and in His arms I lay.
Although dangers surround me, He watches night and day
Protects me from the evil one, and with Him I will stay.

In presence of my enemies and those who wish me ill,
He leads me into pastures safe, beside the waters still.
No torment to ensnare me with Jesus by my side,
Within His courts for evermore in safety I abide.

Abundantly He feeds me in presence of my foes
My table He has furnished, my cup it overflows.
Here I have found shelter and here I love to stay.
Goodness and mercy follow me and keep me every day.

The Right Doors

God opens all the right doors
As you journey on life's road.
Don't push too hard and break the lock
Trust Father God alone.

There are so many options
That you may feel are right.
Make sure that everything you do
Is pleasing in His sight.

Old Age

Old age really isn't so bad
If you can keep from being sad
Retain your teeth, not lose your hair
Arrange for regular joint repair.
Sight may dim and hearing fade,
Brain function may not make the grade.
We know the outward man will crumble
And the pride of life will take that tumble,
But the inner man is renewed each day
And that makes everything OK.

The Scarlet Thread

Follow the thread down through history,
Trace the scarlet thread of God's love.
To angels and men it's a mystery,
Why Jesus should come from above.
To lay down His throne and His sceptre
To be born in the humblest abode,
Displaying in fullness the spectra
Of the wonderful light of God's love.

The prophets foretold of this happening,
'Behold, a child shall be born,
And His name will be called Immanuel
God with us, Redeemer and Lord.'
A baby was born in Bethlehem,
Who knew that this was God's plan?
The thing was revealed down the ages,
From Adam the scarlet thread ran.

On and on to the manger
Where Jesus our Saviour was born.
In distress, discomfort and danger
Unwelcomed and shunned by His own.
Yet that scarlet thread ran on to Calvary,
Where He died in my place, for my sin.
He brought forgiveness for you and for me,
Rose again so new life could begin.

So follow the thread down through history,
Trace the scarlet thread of God's love.
To angels and men it's a mystery,
Why Jesus could come from above
To lay down His throne and His sceptre
Be born in the humblest abode.
Displaying in fullness the spectra
Of the wonderful light of God's love.

Tribute To The Shepherd Of The Flock

Always the servant of the Lord
True shepherd to the flock of God.
You knew God's call whilst in your youth
The call to go and spread His truth
He said, 'Son, do you love Me?'
'Lord, You know, my heart You see.'
'Then feed My sheep,' He said to you
And this you never failed to do.

Always there to lead the way,
The Bread of Life you broke each day
Your energies you did not spare
For those God placed within your care.
Life brought is burdens and its woes
Weakness and sickness took its toll,
But ever striving to know God's will
The Light of Life burned brighter still.

Your ministry has never ended
God's precious flock you've always tended.
We came to you for words of wisdom
Your look, your ready smile, known so well.
Earth mourns your loss, it's Heaven's gain
There's no more sorrow, death or pain.
Sun does not rise not does it set
But the Light of Life burns brighter yet.

Anne Voce

I am forty-one years old and suffer from manic depression or bi-polar affective disorder as it is sometimes known these days. I have had this illness since the age of seventeen and have had about seventeen hospital admissions. As part of my therapy I have done creative writing groups which is where I have written a lot of my poetry. I tend to write my poetry for other people or about them, including my mum and dad who have both passed away. I get worse when I suffer a loss like that and my two longest hospital admissions were after they died. I had a boyfriend called Dean who used to inspire me a lot and several of my poems I have written for him. I sent my poem about my dad liking John Thaw to his widow, Sheila Hancock, and she wrote me a lovely letter thanking me. I also sent 'get well' poems to Frank Bruno and Stuart Goddard (Adam Ant) as I could empathise with them suffering from the same illness as me.

I love writing poems and think it's a good way of expressing one's feelings. My favourite is 'Mixed Blessings' probably because it's the first serious attempt I made at writing a poem and it was part of an assignment I was doing on a childcare course. I think it's a good equal opportunities statement as well.

If I'm successful in getting my work published, I would like to dedicate it to the memory of my mum and dad, and also my baby niece, Isabella Maria.

Mixed Blessings

My dad is black, my mum is white,
Why should that give you the right

To call me names and put me down?
I'm just like you except I'm brown.

I have feelings too - you see,
It hurts when people say of me,

'There she is, half-and-half'
And then they have a good old laugh.

I may be half-and-half outside,
But that only gives me pride.

I share two backgrounds of culture and race,
I have a beautiful golden face.

My tastes are varied, peas and rice,
Or fish and chips without any spice.

Reggae music I enjoy,
I can dig a beat like any black boy.

But any music makes me dance,
And if I get just half a chance,

I'll show you how I strut my stuff,
And you don't have to act so tough.

We can dance together and have some fun,
Black and white, everyone.

We can live together, as sisters and brothers,
Whatever the colour of our fathers and mothers.

We are all God's children underneath,
Whatever our colour, creed or belief.

He would want us to live as one,
And follow the example of His Son.

Unselfish and caring to all mankind,
If you do this you will surely find

That the colour of my skin won't matter to you,
The person that I am will shine right through.

And when you become a friend to me,
You can say to the others - 'Can't you see?

She has something to say right out loud'
And I will stand up tall and proud.

'Now I have your attention at last,
I would like to state, I'm not half-caste.

When I was born, God looked down and smiled
At me, His little mixed-race child.'

Cannabis

It's green and is an eight-leafed plant
Some people like to get high on it, but I can't.
It's called several things; marijuana, hash and dope
But although you're not supposed to get hooked, some can't cope.
They go onto heavier drugs and ruin their lives,
Wind up ending things between husbands and wives.
You start off on soft drugs then go on to 'crack'
Before you know it, you're regularly doing 'smack'.
Women sell their bodies to get their 'fix',
Pimps control them to get their kicks,
Sharing needles can lead to HIV
Then AIDS which ends in death and misery.
Smoking dope may look cool but it's not for me,
I value my right to choose . . . for my sanity.
Pop stars may write about it and also partake -
But in the end the dealers are always on the make.

Mum And Dad

Mum, you've been gone now for two years,
And although I still haven't shed any tears,
I still think and speak of you every day,
Remembering all the laughter we shared along the way.
Now you're reunited with Dad whom we all miss too,
And I feel like he's watching over us, with you.
I know you'd both be pleased about me moving on,
It's taken a long time since you've been gone.
I miss you, Mum and Dad, with all my heart,
It's been a difficult time since you did depart,
But I know when God's ready, I'll be up there with you,
Until then my love for you both will shine through.

My Mum

I was born on Mother's Day 1963,
My dad held me on his knee.
The doctor thought he'd have a laugh -
My dad might have worn a silk scarf.
Trials and tribulations there have been many over the years
And there has been many a time when we've all been in floods of tears.
But Mum you've been there, to comfort and care,
And I know forever you'll always be there -
Your anniversary means memories of 40 loving years -
When we go to Dad's tree, I hope no tears.

The Pot Of Gold At The End Of The Rainbow

There are many sad things happened to me over the years,
Enough to make you scream and cry lots of tears.
But through it all a light shines on me,
Guiding me towards my eventual destiny.

First there was Tom, my first real sweetheart,
Then Dad, then Mum - all of which broke my heart.
But whether this illness paints everything in colours deep and true,
Or if, Dean, it's how much I'm in love with you,

I know that there's a pot of gold at the end of the rainbow,
And together, Babe, we'll find it one day I know.

They say that every cloud has a silver lining,
Well just like my gold I wear, your love keeps me shining.

Tom's Birthday

Today, 10th December 2003 would have been Tom's birthday.
If he were alive I would say, 'Hip hip hooray!'
He lived in Greenwich, No 1 Lockyer House OHB,
I really loved him and he did me.
I still remember his beautiful brown eyes smiling at me,
He had had a hard life that I could clearly see -
He tried to drown away the hurt by drinking and smoking too much,
But all he really needed was a warm and gentle touch.
That I gave him for nearly a year
But now sometimes I still shed a tear,
For he's not here anymore but I still love him in my heart,
For he's gone, not forgotten, and I wish he didn't depart.

The Seasons

In America, they call autumn 'The Fall',
This is the season I like best of all -
Crunching the leaves as they lie on the ground -
It really does make a wonderful sound!
Winter brings thoughts of Christmas and New Year,
With all those warming 'cups of cheer'.
I love Christmas and the snow,
But it gets so cold - don't you know?
Humans should be like squirrels and hibernate,
Just come out for Christmas and New Year to celebrate!
I love spring and summer too -
Going on holiday - maybe somewhere new.
Spring has Easter with chocolate and chicks,
But more importantly remembering the crucifix.
Each season has a magic of its own, I find -
And so shall it be till the end of time.

Why Do We Need A `White Riot`?

Adolf Hitler and Eva Braun were lovers,
But that's nothing to do with our fathers and mothers.

If there's an anti-Christ rising, he'll be born 5.6.56
But that is the same birthdate as my big brov Chris.

He's the kindest, gentlest person you could ever meet
He can play guitar brilliantly - heavy rock - or soft and sweet.

Alright now by Free, Sultans of Swing by Dire Straits
And as for me, The Clash used to be my mates.

What about Sean Purcell and the cuddly toys?
Although they were 'raped' they played a bloody good noise.

I was a regular - Camden Music Machine
But now I'm in love with my boyfriend Dean.

We just want to be soft and cuddly too
And tell each other 'I love you'.

White bears with hearts doing the can-can,
And bags of peanut M&Ms singing 'Stan'.

As Roger Daltry sang 'Hope I Die Before I Get Old'
But now to make my statement - I wear bright and bold.

I am multicoloured - multi racial, and don't feel that old
And from now on it's B&H for me, cos I'm 'Pure Gold'!

Air On A G String (Bach)

Classical music reminds me of my mum and dad.
This piece was definitely among their collection they had.

Dad was an expert on classical music and opera as well
He was intelligent as well, as I think you can tell.

He and Mum passed their intelligence on to me
Between them both, they helped me see

Not all music has to be noisy and loud -
My knowledge now would make them proud,

They took me to concerts from an early age
They were even thinking of putting me on the stage.

I remember them both fondly in everything I do,
And can I just say, 'Mum and Dad

I love you.'

For Frank Bruno

Dear Frank, I'm just writing this poem to say,
That soon you'll be back to A1 OK.
I know what it's like to feel how you do,
I've been there myself but now I've pulled through.
Just want to let you know everyone's thinking of you,
And that there is light at the end of the tunnel too.
If ever you feel up to dropping me a line,
I'd be pleased to hear from you any time.

John Thaw

My dad loved John Thaw,
My mum thinks he's a bore!
My dad loved Inspector Morse -
I do too, but my mum thinks he's morose!
'Sweeney Todd', the flying squad, a long time ago
            with Dennis Waterman,
They were my heroes years ago but a bit violent for me, Anne.
'Goodnight Mister Tom' was the best,
Under the little boy's vest were scars, which made all viewers
            say, 'Aahhh!'
'Kavanagh QC' and 'Home to Roost' -
The comedy side always gives me a boost.
Classical music and crosswords too -
I've made cakes in the shape of them for me and you.
Dad, you were the best in the world,
September the 11th will be sad -
But I'll never forget you, I love you Dad.

Congratulations!

My sis, you've made me very proud,
I want to shout it right out loud!
Making me an aunty once again -
With Isabella next in line to Ben.
Can't wait to see the both of you
And Carol, lots of love to you.
Rest up and take good care,
With your beautiful motherly grace and fair hair.
Can't wait to see you when I can -
Yet again congratulations from big sis Anne

The Moon And New Zealand

I often sit and wonder what it would be like to go to the moon -
If money were no object, I would go there soon.
I'd only take my beloved boyfriend, Dean, with me,
But then I'd come back to New Zealand for the sea!
Backwards and forwards, twice a year at least -
And wherever we'd go, I would cook a feast!
Roast beef on Sundays with home-made Yorkshire pud,
Cakes on birthdays, as I know I could.
When babies come along, we'll treasure them with all our heart,
And know in our hearts we'll never part.
We've been with each other through thick and thin,
Although I've been married before, I know this can't be a sin -
To love someone as I love Dean,
And to know that he is just as keen -
Puts a spring in my step and a smile on my face,
Just waiting for his phone call keeps me in my place!
I love him more as each day goes by,
And know he'll never try to make me cry.

Manic Depression

My illness makes me have highs and lows,
Although why I have it, it seems no one knows.
Now I'm extremely happy, then I'm terribly sad.
It can make me feel up and down which is sometimes bad.
Children I would love one day, but don't want to pass it on,

Doing what I can to keep myself well - needs to be done.
Every time I have a relapse, I tell myself it's the last,
Perhaps this one is it, but it's come back in the past.
Recognising my own signs certainly helps a lot,
Even though sometimes, I feel like just a dot!
'Surely you can't be serious?' I am serious - and don't call me Shirley!
Sometimes I remember Mum saying, 'Call me anything except early!'
I swing a lot, but more up than down,
On my forehead is hardly ever a frown,
Now I know Dean and I are one, I can swim anywhere I like and
                        know I won't drown.

I'll Be Waiting

My heart was thumping as you stood in the dock,
I wasn't sure if you would get a shock -
Seeing me sitting there looking at you
But at least I managed to mouth 'I love you'.
Four months will pass in no time -
Then at last you will be mine,
It may even get reduced to a shorter while -
Then on March 24th we can celebrate in style!
I'll be 40 and you'll be out -
That will be something to shout about!
Seeing you standing there made me realise
Just how much I want to be with you for the rest of our lives.
Dean, I love you more than anything in this world
And you make me so proud to be your girl.

Richele

I once knew a little girl called Richele,
Who was bright as a button and looked like Tinkerbell.

She shone like the sun and I was mates with her mum,
Her little sis was Rosie and she would never smack her bum.

We went to Margate two weeks after we met,
Poor little Richele had never got wet.

She wanted to go on the merry-go-round,
For longer than she was meant to, but what I then found,

Was for me it was a pleasure, to take Richele there,
With her beautiful bright eyes and lovely fair hair.

At the end of the day she cried and cried,
Because she wanted to take the sea home from the seaside!

Mum

Mum, you were always my best friend,
I loved you right up until the end.
You gave so much of yourself to me,
Taught me how to feel loved and free.
Free from the prejudices of my mental health,
What you gave to me was more valuable than wealth.
You were always there for me in person and on the phone,
You never treated my illness as something unknown.
You were my rock until you died three years ago,
And Mum, I love and miss you so.

For Dean

You saw me at the bus stop and asked me for a drink,
My bus was due so I had to stop and think.
You wanted me to come, not go home on my own,
So you offered to pay for my cab home.
Although we spent less than an hour together, it felt right,
And I was pleased when you arrived the following night.
Disappointed to have missed you phoning twice on Friday,
I left a message to say where I'd be on Saturday.
We didn't spend much time together on our own,
But I still didn't want to leave you to go back home.
When we kissed each other, my heart missed a beat,
And now I can't wait for the next time we meet.

Andrew Usher David

I am a Jesus believer. I am not religious, just a simple man of faith. I am 23 years old and I live in East London at the moment; I used to be a chef, then a care worker, now I am a writer. I am also interested in psychology.

I have many other interests and writing poetry is just one of them. I enjoy watching movies, black theatre, sex, world music, reading and singing. I started to write poetry two years ago when I was diagnosed with a mental illness, but now I have fully recovered.

Selections of these poems are taken from my second anthology, 'Silent Echoes from the Soul'. The poems are about soul-searching, identity and spirituality.

Since I started writing poetry, I have been on a journey and I've learnt a lot about myself from reading my own poetry; my inspirations come from God, people and life in general. I was an emotionally complicated person who had struggled with identity and had no one to direct me in life until Jesus showed me the way. Now I'm a more mature and balanced person with purpose in my life, and all my poetry reflects that journey.

I am blessed to have the chance to share my poetry and I'd like to thank 'Spotlight Poets' for another opportunity.

I have beaten all the odds against me and I have only done that because of my faith. I would like to encourage anybody who has talents to use them even if you have a disability and no one believes in you; believe in yourself and you'll be surprised at what you can achieve.

The world is your oyster.

Have You Seen?

Have you seen?
The other side of me,
The bitterness and anger,
The sunken ship under the sea.
Have you seen?
Underneath my skin.
The carelessness and foolishness,
The enemy within.
Have you seen?
The times I was wrong,
Believing in people,
Singing the same old song.
Have you seen?
My simple heart break,
The dysfunctional me,
The pills I take.
Have you seen?
When I wear a disguise,
If you haven't,
Open your eyes.

Identity

Never run away from who you are,
Whether you're right or wrong,
Face up to your identity,
And soon it won't be long.
All the doors will open,
And your happiness shall begin,
A new window will open
So shine your light from within.
Use your time wisely,
And you will surely see,
Love others while you can,
Love is the only key,
To unlock your identity,
To open your heart,
To love someone who loves you,
You are now on the right path.

Open Me

Open me,
Like you open a book,
Come inside and take a look.

Open me,
Like a can of drink,
And watch everything pour out,
Open me,
Like you open your mouth,
And hear the words come out,
Open me,
Like you open a gift,
And see everyone gather round,
Open me,
Like you open a carcass,
And expect to hear the vultures' sound.

Open me,
Like you open a book
Come inside if you dare,
And take a good look.

Hidden Treasure

Face your destiny,
Face yourself,
There is only you,
There is nobody else.
Search your heart,
Look inside your soul,
There you'll find power,
Now take control.
Look to the future,
Don't turn around,
Now you'll see what has been waiting for you,
The hidden treasure you have found.

Living Waters

Living waters,
Sprinkling over my soul,
Healing every broken wound,
Refilling every deep hole.
Streams of life,
Now flowing through my veins,
I have so much to live for,
New experiences to gain.
Whoever gave me this water?
Pouring till my glass overflows,
Please quench my every thirst,
And satisfy this soul.

I Am

I am an individual,
I am eccentric and loud,
I am eclectic in every way,
I am not just a face in the crowd.
I am not a stereotype,
I am not to be compared,
I am not afraid to be different,
I am not offended if you stare.
I am a light in this world,
I am the salt of the earth,
I am a child of the living God,
I am the new birth.

Soldier

I am a soldier,
With every weapon at hand,
Marching on in all power,
Making a difference,
In any way I can.
Covered in armour,
From head to toe,
Exposing all powers of darkness,
Wherever I go.
Sword and shield,
A word and a blow,
The world is my arena,
I am now on show.
Friends in high places,
My position is secure,
My enemies are beneath me,
Death is no longer at my door.

You

My inspiration comes from you,
You are my light, you are my truth.
Nothing exists unless you say,
Because of you I wake up every day.
You are my honey, you are my flower,
You are my energy source, my only power.
You are the door of my peace,
Because of you my soul is at ease.
You hold the keys to paradise,
You are the medicine for my pain,
You are my island in the sun,
In the desert you are my rain.
You are the one, who knows my name,
Because of you I will never be ashamed.

The Small Still Voice

Words without faith are useless.
Wisdom and understanding are
The bearers of truth.
The truth can set you free from your oppression,
From your depression.
Dealing with the obstacles will create
Hope and honesty in yourself.
Believe in me, free yourself,
Listen to me.

Listen to the small still voice,
Not the one in your head,
But in your spirit instead.
Keep away from evil,
Do not associate with trees that bear the wrong fruit.
Surround yourself with positive things.
Read these instructions,
And listen to know understanding.
Eternal life is granted to those who believe in me.
So obey my commandments in this life.

Your Love

Your love is like a shelter,
When there is no one else around,
Your love is like gravity,
Pulling me safely to the ground.
Your love is like water,
Soothing the deepest part of me,
Your love is like a sword,
Piercing right through the heart of me.

Your love is like a dove,
Peaceful, gentle and kind,
Your love is like a lamp,
Guiding me when I am blind.

The sparkle in your eyes,
Lights the fire in my soul,
Your beautiful smile, your sweet embrace,
Keeps me warm whenever I am cold.
Your love is like a key,
Your love has set me free,
Your love is like a drug,
Your love is all I need.

It's My Life

It's my life,
I have learned to accept,
No one there to control me,
I have no regrets.
More baggage has been lifted,
Including some who called themselves friends,
I have no time for shallow, negative people,
So I am on my own again.
I am back in the driver's seat,
Slowly moving forward every day,
No one here to stop me,
I'm ignoring every delay.
No more asking for help,
As I always have to pay.
I have learnt to love myself,
I don't have time for anyone else,
No one really knows me,
Maybe no one ever will,
It's only my life,
So I'll choose to live, still.

This World

This world I live in,
Is the world I hate,
This evil system,
A crazy fake.

My home is not of this world,
But somewhere far,
A beautiful place beyond the furthest star.
This world I live in,
A place of distress,
A jungle full of monkeys,
People made up in fancy dress.

This world I live in,
A web of illusion,
A box of secrets and lies,
A maze of entrapment and confusion.
This world I live in,
Used to be paradise in the sun,
Now a place filled with darkness,
With nowhere to run.

This world I live in,
Is the world I hate,
This evil system,
I have no place.

The Runway

The runway is clear,
I see the open road,
I see no more stop signs,
My vision has lightened the load.
Travelling to the unknown,
A journey to the other side,
Not taking in anymore hitchhikers,
Only moving forward only to find,
That the runway is narrower,
Than the one I left behind.
The past is still behind me,
As far as I can see,
The runway, on which I am travelling,
Can only lead to my destiny.

A

A shining light,
A dark blue night,
A pathway to eternity,
Where angels take flight.
A bridge over water,
A hole in the storm,
A melody for the soul,
Where a fire keeps you warm.
A friend to talk to,
A shoulder for the tears,
A lonely life to walk through,
A cross I have to bear.

Thank You Jesus

Thank You Jesus,
For everything You've done,
For bringing joy and laughter,
I now shine like the sun.
Thank You Jesus,
From the bottom of my heart,
For placing Your spirit within me,
For giving me a new start.
Thank You Jesus,
For being my father, my mother,
For being a shoulder to lean on,
For also being my brother.
Thank You Jesus,
For being my umbrella,
A shelter in the storm,
From all kinds of weather.
Thank You Jesus,
For lifting me up every day,
For being my comforter, my guide,
For showing me the way.
Thank You Jesus,
For teaching me how to pray,
Thank You Father,
Thank You Spirit,
Thank You Jesus,
Is all that I can say.

Forget

Forgetting the past,
It's so hard to do,
Especially when you've made it through,
Yet no one can see it except for you.
People, they say nothing new,
Even when I'm happy,
They make me blue,
Yet they try to stick to me like glue.
I laugh when they patronise me,
To make themselves feel better,
Reminding me of what they think I lack,
The things I have chosen to forget forever.
Still they cannot keep me down,
It's not because of them I'm no longer bound.
It's only because I choose to forget,
That I can now face each new day without regret

Stephen Humphries

I am a forty-three-year-old Irishman living in Spain. I left Ireland over twenty years ago, going to sea with the merchant navy. I spent three years in the navy, travelling the world. I then travelled by myself working on a variety of jobs in a number of countries.

By chance rather than design, I found myself in Spain and for the last sixteen years I've lived on the island of Mallorca with my Basque wife. I'm self employed, working in the yachting industry, mostly shore-based now but I still take the occasional trip back to sea when circumstances allow.

I began writing about three or four years ago and really enjoy it. It is my dream to be a full-time professional writer. To date I've written three novels, though have yet to succeed in having any of them published. I also write short stories, poetry and plays, and I've enjoyed more success with these.

I find poetry very enjoyable and try to convey a message in each poem. Some are a political comment on life in general while others take a more personal look at life. Some poems have a humorous theme, giving a wry look on everyday life, recurring themes such as hope, life, chance and scepticism reflect the mood, often with a healthy dose of irreverence and cynicism. I find that I can express a sentiment in a poem that sometimes escapes me in discussion with others.

Darkness

Dark thoughts,
In a darkened room,
A light is cast,
Into the gloom.
Dark reflections,
On an empty life,
A time gone by,
Lost in the night.
Remembering times,
That now seem sad,
Of missed opportunities,
In a life gone mad.
Times once good,
May come again,
And light may enter,
This dark den.
Tomorrow's stars,
May shine like before,
And leave this gloom,
For evermore.
Darkest nights,
Hold no fears,
Tomorrow's light,
Will find me here.

Time

Give me time,
Give me motion,
But what to do?
I have no notion.
I've seen enough,
To find my way,
I've had my chance,
I've had my say.
Yet in my head,
There's no solution,
In my life,
There's just confusion.
Which direction?
Which road to take?
A life that's real?
Or one that's fake?
Too many questions,
For me to answer,
I lead a life,
Of a merry chancer.
Give me time,
And make it last,
No more mistakes,
That's in the past.
A second chance,
To right the wrong,
And finally rest,
It's been so long.

An Evening Still

A peaceful calm,
Like a gentle chill,
Descends around us,
Our minds to fill.
A gentle sigh,
Escapes our lips,
A time to rest,
From weary trips.
A quiet time,
The air so still,
Idle hours,
And time to kill.
To close one's eyes,
The tension gone,
And in its place,
A half-remembered song.
Humming softly,
A smile suppressed,
We count our blessings,
And take our rest.
Reflecting back,
On roads we took,
On names and faces,
And slices of luck.
A twisted journey,
Of chance and thrill,
Relived in seconds,
On an evening still.

From Time To Time

All your life,
You do your best,
Work hard for pennies,
That you invest.
The years roll by,
The pennies grow,
You hope in time,
You've something to show.
But from time to time,
You often wonder,
Is this the way?
Or do I blunder?
All the years,
Of scrimp and save,
To the mighty clock,
A daily slave.
When I'm old,
Or so they tell me,
I'll have no cares,
Or woes to fell me.
But from time to time,
I do insist,
I want to live,
Not just exist.
So give me the pennies,
Tomorrow can wait,
And to hell with the clock,
I'm out that gate!

A Second Coming

He sends a message,
We listen clear,
It's information,
We need to hear.
It's up to date,
On the situation,
But the message is lost,
In translation.
He's coming back,
So make some plans,
To pacify,
The hostile lands.
He'll make some changes,
Let's be frank,
He'll probably start,
With the Vatican bank.
A lot of things,
Done in His name,
Yet goodwill to man,
Is not in the frame.
Corruption is rife,
People are dying,
Trouble and strife,
And the children crying.
What's the solution?
Gentile and Jew?
History repeated,
They learned what to do.
The Holy Land,
A place of hate,
A Second Coming,
May have to wait.

A Dream Alive

A dream alive,
A beautiful thought,
Hard pressed by doubt,
A refuge is sought.
This dream alive,
Will keep you going,
When hope fades pale,
And weakness showing.
Believe the plan,
Believe the dream,
The time has come,
And you must scheme.
Bide your time,
Ignore the noise,
One eye on the money,
One on the prize.
The time has come,
To make your move,
To trust yourself,
Nothing left to prove.
Pick the moment,
That's hard to find,
The worry and doubt,
Left behind.
This dream alive,
Is not for sale,
A price too high,
For a soul to fail.

Life's Journey

Life's a journey,
With many starts,
To see new things,
Follow new charts.
Different places,
Different times,
Different customs,
Different signs.
Seek the knowledge,
Share the wealth,
Record the memories,
Preserve the health.
Life's a journey,
With roads to take,
To learn new things,
And make mistakes.
Chances to weigh,
Decisions to take,
Learn right from wrong,
For goodness sake.
Hope that in time,
You'll see the day,
You'll have earned your lines,
Accepted your grey.
Hope that the person,
Who started the trip,
Has spent their time well,
By the sun's final dip.

At Water's Edge

At water's edge,
A river flowing,
A smouldering mass,
Of energy growing.
Endless motion,
The cycle be,
From mountain peak,
Down to the sea.
Beneath the surface,
A current swift,
At journey's end,
A tidal drift.
Along its banks,
Life goes on,
From rural field,
To city and town.
A silent witness,
To all humanity,
The smog and noise,
And sheer insanity.
Its water gives,
A chance of life,
To those who wade,
Through daily strife.
At water's edge,
Life goes on,
An endless cycle,
From dusk to dawn.

Come The Morrow

Late at night,
With time to kill,
Reflecting back,
On life so still.
The heat of the day,
Gone for now,
And in its place,
A silent vow.
Come the morrow,
Come the day,
To do things better,
In every way.
The past is gone,
No regrets, no fear,
It won't be long,
'Til tomorrow is here.
Hear the silence,
Hear the past,
Leave it behind,
Where shadows are cast.
A time to reflect,
On what might have been,
Fate's fickle hand,
The future unseen.
Hear the night,
And sleep in peace,
Tomorrow is ours,
Our fears can cease.

Louise Vincent

I was born in Swindon, Wiltshire, on December 29th 1983. My family spent a brief period of time abroad in Algeria where my father worked. Before my youngest brother was born, I, my eldest brother and my mother moved back to the UK.

In December 1993, my father was tragically killed while still in Algeria. With my life completely changed, I concentrated on my schoolwork. The only reward from that was five years of bullying. It was during this period that I discovered my love for English literature, reading and writing.

With a friend, we tried to work on various writing projects although they never really amounted to anything, but it was the experience that counted. I continue to work on various projects of my own, one of which started out as a journal but has grown over the years.

Before I left Sixth Form in 2002, I showed some of my poetry to my English teacher who introduced me to Forward Press. This lead to one of my poems, 'Falling' being published in a 'Women's Words' anthology.

I spent the last two summers working at a Girl Scout camp in Minnesota through Camp America. It completely opened my eyes to the different people and their lives and also the lives of the girls I looked after. I made friends there that I know will last a lifetime and that will always be there for me.

As I grow older I hope to use my writing as a way of raising awareness in adults as to how children cope with tragedy and torment in their lives, especially bullying.

Falling

For years I have wondered will life ever change?
Will things ever stop feeling so strange?
It's been so long now and still I cannot forget,
The feeling I felt, the feeling that came out.

It's been so long now and still it hurts,
Hurts so bad even I cannot work.
Concentration seems to fail,
As I fall deeper into my own personal hell.

This falling I cannot control,
It has a hold only time will tell,
I need to fight but somehow cannot,
For this hold has a force even I forgot.

Tearful Hopes

As I stand here wondering why
A tiny tear falls from my eye
My life has changed so suddenly
My body shakes uncontrollably.

Why I know what I do
Is beyond me and you too
You left my life causing pain
I pray and hope but it stays the same.

As I stand here wondering why
I realise I cannot change my life
Since you left there has been pain
Please come back and make me whole again.

Careless

Nobody cares or decides to notice
How life can pass by so careless and fast
But some believe 'Hey you only live once'
We're given one chance to make it last.

Some people want to savour the moment
But have it snatched so nastily away
Thoughts of others I have tried to change
But for now we live with their mistakes every day.

Decision

I've taken my time
And now decided to draw the line
I've had enough
Stuff everything I've given up.
You've tormented my life
Caused so much pain and strife
I've drawn the line
You've run out of time.

Untitled

Mountains tall and never-ending
Hopes of love I keep on sending
Wondering why I feel so alone
Need someone to call my own

Green meadows wide and vast
Will this feeling always last?
Need to find that special person
Need the friendship of something certain

Winter rivers weary and sad
When really I am around nothing bad
People come and go from my strife
Those who are my friends for life.

Memories Of An Innocent

Gentle warm breeze holds you in its embrace,
The little flutter of your black lace,
You remember the day when it went cold and harsh,
The day you thought you could no longer last.

Pain continued through all your days,
Hurt, anger, stress and fear followed on in different ways,
All these feelings bottled up causing you strife,
Wish upon wish that you could end your life.

Knife in hand and thoughts in head,
Wanting to cut to end this dread,
Knowing really that life will never stay the same,
These feelings rushed out releasing your pain.

Years have gone by now and although it still hurts,
The pain has eased and life has its flirts,
You remember the day so clear in your mind,
But you must move on now and leave it behind.

Heartless

We met like strangers
Eyes across a crowded room
Maybe it just wasn't meant to be

I tore my heart up in my own hands
Broken whatever could have been
Again I saw myself all alone

Years pass by so fast and slow
Still I lie here all alone.

American Dream

I made the choice to go away,
Leave behind what I knew best,
Travelled a distance to make the heart sway,
Then I came to rest.

Did not know where I was headed,
Did not know who was around.

For this summer I want you to know
That I thank each and every one of you,
You've made my life so much more
With experiences and adventures all the days through.

Reliving

Once again I find myself standing here, alone
Do you remember the visions of a place we used to call home?
And now it's like I'm breathing for the first time again
And now it's like I'm seeing remnants of an old friend

Places, memories and shattering dreams
All come back reminding me of you
The life I've chosen so far away
From where I am now I need to stay
Close yet far and I'm back in a bar
On West 7th Street with old friends

Years of pain and hurt return,
I've paid my price and now it's done.

Drama

How could life change so dramatically?
Why would these things torture me?
I have no control of my own life
Please, I need help, some relief from this night.

Darkness engulfs every cornerstone
I hide in the shadows hoping someone will come
The help I seek never seems to appear
Why does life treat me with such revere?

Memories replay like my own cinema,
Thinking of ways that could change my life,
How did it end up that I was so out of control?
How did my choices destroy my soul?

Life, it seemed like such a game,
Moments and questions never grasped
They float around this empty space,
Unanswered moments haunt my mind.

Forever Friend

You know when I'm sad or happy
You know how to put a smile on my face
One look at you my heart melts
Time and time again.

I watch you just being, knowing that it will end
Knowing that some day
I will lose my truest friend.

Friendship

Friends are forever, nothing else is simpler
You've stood by me, through every moan and whimper
You've stuck up for me when things were tough
You've been my pillar when times were rough

You somehow understood me, my confused little mind
Being caring and friendly instead of leaving me blind
Now I want to say, 'Thank you' ever so much
I hope this friendship lasts no matter what.

Don't Worry

The whisper of a breath
So gentle on your skin
Scenery that matches your face
Nowhere, no place
Could be as cold as this

You treat her like she's not worth
The love every human deserves
She feels the same time after time
Each excuse you give her
She believes even more than before.

Survival

Is my life really worth it?
The hassle of the daily grind
Is there point and purpose
To suffering in our lives?

What stops a person
From making that fatal cut?
What stops a person
From swallowing that fatal pill?

Everyone survives
In certain and different ways
Why can I not do the same?
Survival seems to fade.

Through The Eyes Of . . .

Razor-sharp blade cuts through their life
Poisoned beliefs of what might be right
Families' anger and lovers' strife
Yet another death to hear of tonight

The world has changed or so we thought
It's not such a different story
No lessons learned as once was said
The old lie of . . .
Dulce et decorum est pro patria mori

Arthur Greenwood

I was born in Belfast in January 1951. It was the 13th and my mother used to hint that it was a Friday. Before the age of five, my father's job forced a move to Portadown in County Armagh and subsequently I went to school at St Patrick's College in Armagh City. I think that I was extremely fortunate to have been educated by the Vincentians for they encouraged a very liberal and optimistic outlook on all subject areas. I left there in the late sixties and progressed through Queen's University Belfast taking a degree in Dentistry. I had remained a 'tooth jockey' for thirty years until ill health forced me to retire prematurely in 2003. In the early part of my career I co-wrote a number of research papers and I suppose that sparked an interest in writing and indeed in reading, mostly science fiction and poetry. My favoured poets include Seamus Heaney, Michael Longley, John Montague and a former school acquaintance, Paul Muldoon. My ambition is to be able to write poetry which is readable, understandable and enjoyable, like that of my favourites. I have had two poems published; 'The Appointment Card' and 'Are You Hearing This?' and two others have been selected for publication, 'Bequia' and 'School Yard'. All I need now is a smiling God.

Adventure In Aruba

Down, down, down through the heaving sea.
'Thus Zarathrustra Spake' finaled
As we touched the seabed
In a sprinkle of sand-sea spray
And settled in wonder, safely
Placed in this metal balloon,
Gazing, open-mouthed, at the
Like-minded shoals and schools
Of different coloured shapes
That gaped back, open-mouthed,
At the different coloured shapes
Inside the yellow box.
Forward slowly, passed a wreck,
Recently descended remnant of
Some collision with the medium
In which we moved so smoothly.
And then around the coral,
Spectacular and vibrant, as
The sun dipped its yellow finger
And stroked this living wonder.
Now astern, retraced our path,
Ensuring the ascent to just
The proper place where we embarked.

Daffodil

Spring's southern balm caresses
The white ground-sheet of winter
And gently peels this crisp cover
Revealing grass and soil and flower.

The hardy yellow cup reflects
The solar glow and kindles
Primal joy and hope of
New birth and life and kin.

And when the winter closes
Down on souls a daffodil
Casts shadow on their path,
A sign of certain re-awakening.

Stone Walls

Stinging grains of sand sculpt weather-beaten skin.
He tries to shelter from the screaming sea-wind,
Standing wet-footed in the sodden peat,
Balancing another stone between hands and knee.

The mason wipes salty tears from his nose
And quints towards the master's house,
Fearful of the biting hose
That cuts the back skin loose.

Pennies paid to build these walls
To purchase rotting tubers mixed with grass,
Some filling for the empty bellies,
Some food to break the murderous fast.

And death will come anyway;
Not enough stones to stay the scythe,
To hold the Reaper back.
The builder puts his thoughts aside.

That cold Atlantic breath, wet and hostile,
Does not deter him from his bleeding task,
For he will die here serving time
To squeeze the gold for those who ask.

White Water: Pacuare, Costa Rica

Surly, shaven trees, upturned branches like
hands pressed against sodden faces,
witness our irreverent entrance,
giggling, going through our paces as we launch the blue raft
dropping into the white horses
that slap at the beaten banks,
exposing blocks of ancient rock.
Our boat turns and churns, twirling us, swirling us downstream
and, escaping through angry rapids, comes to rest on stones which burn
our feet on stepping ashore.
We gasp for breath, we gasp for more
time to stay at rest on dry earth.
This earth that swallowed
rain for days and, overburdened,
filled this river to engorgement,
trailing down the sullen trees
and driving shanty towns below
the chopping, slopping waves which we had skimmed over
and whooped and laughed in selfish isolation.

There Is No Answer To That

What should I take
Through the eight foot drop?
Will my thoughts disappear?
Will my consciousness stop?

Who will be with me
On the other side?
Shall I have words to say?
Will I know that I've died?

Will I still see you
When I've gone away?
Will I be in your thoughts
Every time that you pray?

Will I meet any family
Or friends over there?
Will I have time to spend?
Will I have time to care?

And what of all that
I've learnt in life?
Will it be dismissed?
All erased in a trice?

The Eve Of Hallowmas

The soft October rain dampened clothes and sounds
And forced the chimney smoke to seek escape
Along the route through alleys where our thoughts
Of spies and pirates and jewel thieves were halted
As we slipped and tripped on sodden leaves
Which folded in against the walls.

That sulphur taste dried in my throat and made me
Hurry in to wonder at the sights and sounds
Which Uncle Sam had purchased on his way from work
And as we drank our lemonade we watched the rockets
Zipping skywards and the Roman candles pulsing
And the Catherine wheels revolving and the sparklers fading out.

Apple tart and ice cream tasted so much sweeter
When my teeth could feel the hardness of the tanner or the shilling
And then across the road to Harry's with a spending resolution
To add a liquorice whirl or pipe to my provisions
And he would ask me in to join the fray of cousins
Dunking apples in the backroom near the kitchen.

Sniffling in the mizzle I waited at the stop
Until the red tram trundled towards me
To offer entrance through the open rear door
Guarded by the whistling tram conductor who leaned against the stairs
Which spiralled up to fearsome heights where older people
            Smoked and prayed that all was well on Hallowe'en

Schemer-Redeemers

Did we invite this evil to our land
To give us back our freedom and our dignity?
To take away the terror and the crushing hand
Of leadership so blighted, so infused with tyranny?

Must we be forced to welcome such a band
Of barely-adult, left-school-early heroes?
Who do not care, nor think, nor understand
Our aspirations, our desire for peace not haloes?

And give them water, wine or cups of tea,
And shake their hands and kiss their cheek?
But when they turn their eyes and see
That maybe some of us are not so meek,

They change the mood that brought them smiles
And point their guns at us in fear,
As if we could betray them or deny the miles
That they have travelled bringing aid to here.

Our sons and fathers dragged back into camps
That tyrant built to guarantee his power,
And chained and beaten, pulled across the ramps,
Tethered to the walls and made to cower.

These scenes on millions of domestic screens,
The valiant seen, not what they seem,
And leaders plead that this which is obscene,
Is not their plan, not what they mean.

So we look on and ask ourselves again,
Why did we welcome help from such a tribe?
For whilst we tried to bear our previous pain,
We could not know that we would lose our pride.

Not Just Vision

Practise listening to the news,
Helps me differentiate the blues,
Divide them into different hues.
Helps me pick a pair of shoes.

Licking all my favourite greens
Helps me quantify the beans,
Divide them into different streams.
Helps me see what stays unseen.

Sniffing all the yellow flowers
Helps me trickle down the hours,
Scent of grass in April showers
Helps me graduate my colours.

Holding eyelids tightly closed
Lets me sometimes be disposed
To see what oranges and red
Are really like and not just said.

Fondling silks and wool and linen
I realise what I've been given.
Knowing I can feel the living
Other people only see.

I Remember

I remember that very hot morning when the plane bumped down
On the runway and the searing heat on my face coming down
The aircraft steps and the sight of a tall, very dark, out of place
Guy with a tweed jacket and the gun-oil leaving a trace
On the back of it, and the way he escorted us down through
The row of parked motorbikes and police cars and the twisting
Blue tops and the sirens wailing endlessly . . .
I don't remember you standing in front of those guys
And stopping their insults with your disarming smiles.
I don't remember you putting your arms around me and
Helping me on to the bus, shielding me from the abuse
And stinging words, and taking me home and
Washing my face and head.
I don't remember you checking my hands and feet and . . .

Hands

Hands mark time, one rushing past the other.
Hands mark time, one writing about a mother.
Hands held out, giving and taking.
Hands held out, sleeping and waking.
Hands, wringing and tense.
Hands, forgiving, immense.
Hands caressing,
Hands confessing.

School Yard

Crunching through the reddened leaves
The shrieks of innocent playful banter
Drew me back to when I went down slides
And played upon the swings
And then I saw the cars and the
Parents waiting nervously
To usher home their little charges.
There were no cars waiting when I left school
No worries disturbed my parent's peace.
But now each caring mum and dad
Is fearful of the playground beast.

Dominica, Nature's Secret

A poet welcomed us ashore
To 'Nature's Little Secret' isle,
His lyrics charmed our quizzing souls
To linger long, to stay a while.

We took a jeep to view the gendered waterfalls
Over rough terrain and past 'The Pit',
Ascending through the forest trail
And then on foot, we slipped and tripped
And wondered at the green umbrella
Which shielded us from heavy showers,
And underfoot, bright yellow crabs
Scuttled quickly, seeking shelter
From our intrusive steps
That took us to the platform
From which we watched the roaring water
Diving into churning, foaming pools so far below.
And so we turned to our descent,
We passed the locals snapping yams,
Securing calabash to load their vans.
Then onwards through a glade where
Squawking rainbow-coloured parrots
Beaked at tiger caterpillars to
Dislodge them from the broad
Green foliage which they plundered.

The poet bade us adios
And thanked us for our interest
As we embarked our boats
And thanked him for his patience.

Curious Curaçao

Analgesic pastel shades of pink and blue and lemon
Reflect and ripple in the harbour water;
The market shunts and trembles as
Every passing vessel hesitates to view
The to and fro of farmers' fare
As each purveyor jumps from barge to barge.

An outstretched pontoon of wood and steel
Clasps and unclasps, greets and embraces
All who channel into port and
Drop anchor at southern Amsterdam,
And troop ashore to test, compare
This sun-drenched isle with wet and deary motherland.

Breeze From The Southlands

Blanketing northwards I am aware of all my borders
Drawing up the sand along my route
Swirling it underneath my folds
To empty as I pass and leave it underfoot.

Twisting in massive swathes and curls of cloud
Gathering my flocks to keep them safe
Far from footed hunters, I hurl
Them westwards and eastwards and out of harm's way.

And often when I'm cooling down the vapour
Overloading at my edge must fall below
To re-hydrate the dusty scape and liven
Up the colours which camouflage the land.

And then I halt in calm and
Slowly turn and shrink myself through channels
That lead me round again and let me build
And build my power and gather speed
And reappear.

Twelfth Disturbance

Ankles clash bone to bone,
Knees tucked under chin,
Small hands grip the blanket border.
Drums start beating, room becomes yellow,
Dawn just over, sleep disturbed by noise disorder.

Heart-rate quickens, sheet pulled over
Small head, eyes slammed tight, unforced tears
Wet cheeks and dampen cover.
Secret messages from drum to drum
Stir up unknown primal fears.

Childish feet on fresh swept carpet
Tip-toe doorwards seeking solace,
Urging Dad to waken, listen to the drumbeat quicken.
Outstretched arm provides a means
To climb to calming quilt and childish dreams.

Kerri Moore

The 'artist' will never die! His purpose being his striving to exist in relation to his beliefs, as with moment, a provocation of his feelings, a journal of time. Through political systems and agendas, the true eye of communication, the journalist, will always fight to survive, to be understood in a language or pictorial sense, in representative, or mere observation and invention of the subjective/objective narrative of time. And why? A very core being to its existence within a human kind, to aspire to its kindred, a purpose, to bring a truth to expose its own body and soul, its own existence, to an expanse beyond itself, almost a scientist to his word and language, his art.

Even to be a fool in the naiveté of time has its own language, its own beauty. As innocence, in an understanding that its concept will become wise, and yet, it will become a fool again, to wisdom yet uncovered or evolved within our own time systems, that which is to come, will be understood.

And, make of it what we believe! Yet, see unfold truths to which our existence as the human being, can have no effect or relevance within the greater space created by mankind. My poetry unites my being within its own system of explanation and space to become conscious with the use of language.

Language is human kinds only means and tool by which the relevance to the human being can exist. The truth it builds around itself is conscious only to language. To sense anything more, is little less than a guessing game, or 'imagination'. The solidity of language by its existence, is the only means by which we have built truth and being, whether subjective or objective by our agenda, over time and space, perhaps by that, which we can imagine 'the beginning', of sense, communication of sense, and individual/collective consciousness.

In poetry, I was able to capture moment and word of explanation for the heartfelt naiveté and journey from fool, to wise man, to fool again. I found it intriguing, the beauty of language, the truth of its existence, and its possibilities. To admit it little less than an elaborate word play . . . but isn't life?

Love Dancin' In My Shadow

I was askin' to be kissed,
It sure would be all I wished,
More than could be true,
More than I could give a damn.

I'm keeping out of Heaven,
I'm keeping out of Hell,
It could be more than I'm wishing for,
More than I could tell.

Then, in the dance of a shrew,
Came whispers to me,
I did not fear, I did not let loose,
I did not open every door.

My shackle, my shackle,
The love I give to you,
This the heart, this the show, this the love,
Dancing in my shadow.

The spirit dancing in my shadow.

Fanfaronade

The greedy glint of a man,
The bird which lets fly
And grazes upon the feast
Of my face, like an illusion.

Did I embezzle the graceful grackle?
In a rich repose of chatter,
The monumental worship,
The benign renderings, of nonsense.

The oily hues, my past,
The sun drenched hemispheres,
The avenues, our homelands,
In serenades, of sunrise over other lands.

This morning, the sun sings . . .
To the coming of spring,
The yearning of necessity,
To sing his song.

Scratch now at my soul!
Come down the line,
A toreador in the parade of love,
Come pierce me with your vision.

The unlatched tongue, the taste of freedom,
The blushing of aspiring pride,
All inspiring, in longing and immensity,
All my love, and intimate failure.

It is of no matter, now it has gone,
The fancy free realms in tattle,
The criticising of your humble fettle,
May the doves fly about you.

Bid goodbye to reality's farewell,
The light which was but a spark,
Lit the fires, and swept
Through the skies of my heart.

Sepulchre

If I could mast indifference, and make lookout
Of naiveté, I should know all its facets.
Ever to grace its presence,
I observed, in you, and your telling of me,
When wrongly I grieved,
And banished my senses to blushing memory.

How I smiled, with you, within
All my endearing observations,
Which you endured then looked in disbelief -
That I could speak with such belief, not knowing,
How superior I had become in my ignorance
To our dying, with a heavy hand.

How could I deny my life? So reserved
In feeling, I shattered in outburst,
Or forget command to desire
The same of freedom and humanity?
Then sail upon the ebb and flow, and should it reach me,
On the shore, I wait, patiently.

The Astral Body

In the body of a rattlesnake skin,
I fired the revelation
Heavenward,
His primeval paramour,
His Latin conscience.

A raven headed woman,
Spins like a heavenly witch,
Her lineage,
Her renascent,
Redeeming reprise.

She protects many things,
And from her
Demure fingertips,
Comes that moonshine,
In the hail of clarion.

We walked the earth,
Breathed of its flaunting,
Its honeyed flavours,
Plucked of its oysters.
And made charms of its melody.

Will the satellite see its own destruction?

Consign

Gold and silver make of you possessor,
Heavenly and incongruous, the bond
Of faith, flings you like flotsam into space,
The high spirited mansion of prima facie,
Furthermost, from communicant or conceit.

In the holy homeland, the tawdry hubris,
To murmur mulishly of dominion!
To plant the seed and make root;
The passion flower, to expose the crown,
That paid honour, and ousted Christ of life.

And love, who out-bid her equity, howbeit,
The human being, could make bail, privy,
And raise her voice in choirs,
To proclaim, her spoofing wisdom,
Did claim Heaven for her own reward!

Factory Of Dream

The factory swell,
I remember it well,
The homecoming tides,
The despondent.

The iron grey walls,
The emphatic dreams,
The mealy-mouthed
Credit of truth.

The electricity of night,
The bottom of the bottle,
The long kiss goodnight,
A good hiding!

Everyone's heart,
Ripped apart,
The bargain of escape,
The dispossessed.

Thank God,
For Alexander.

Marguerite

Her prosaic liturgies,
Malinger,
Toward the bright side.

Of perdition,
Hors de combat,
Pursuit has no reason.

In my spurring sputter,
Of Marguerite's loveliness,
Her pearls, and seeds.

And her optimism,
Screaming, 'Habdabs,
They are radiant as fish eggs'.

Lacewing

Floss on the eyelids of an angel,
Frost on the delicacy of lacewing,
Cold was his love in delusion,
Icicles from tears of the wind.

The harvest of the holy poet,
Imbued with the candour of light,
Hopes only to shadow devotion,
Help the angel in his flight.

To the luminous consequence,
To miraculous delight,
To elevation and rapture,
The senses seize, recite.

All the sensibilities of an angel,
Though his wings are fettered in ice,
I'll warm him with my potency,
I'll thaw him with my vice.

The Bugle Call

Hunter, hunter!
Did you not convict her?
Of her major tragedies?
And modest gaucherie?
Her mediocre tendencies?

A copperplate gate,
Of Antiquity, to adorn
In her deep impression;
The languor of the winds,
Reedy laudation of stanzas.

Falsehood could plant his seed,
Mummering a bubblin' potion,
In the night, or klutz of dawn.
Wake! We were dreaming.
Misty curtains call.

We make salute.
To Freedom! To dying!
For the cause!
Sing now, morning's glory,
From the darkness of sleep.

To Pedro!

Benedictine,
      My soul!
Demystify my heart,
      My euphoria!
      Evander,
      Thou won the battle.

Maya,
      My instincts!
Betray me now!
      I eat the seeds,
      Of Pinon trees,
      I taste sweet airs.

To Pedro!
To his exile!
To cobalt waters,
Across the deserts,
And other lands.
I drink a cup of heart shape flowers.

The Silent Witness

Intrepid poses of allusive muses,
In maladroit clouds of deposition,
Rake your soul to conclusion.
Peels, the Day of Judgement,
It's devotees in pietistic revulsion,
So speak of shame . . .

Orators redress the onus,
Of integrity, the unimpeachable enmity;
The inviolable shamble of these demigods!
Their demagogues do implore
These dunderheads to denigrate.
To see and believe! In innocence!

Intimate is the nation,
In overdose, and imprisoned,
Its inmates are addressed,
To drape in their personas,
Grateful and genial,
Acquiesced, whether dead or induced.

Nefarious is the consolation,
A malignant point of view!
Man of war! Command to navigate
The malaise, of my quivering
Existence, in opinion,
He secedes to use the manacled vision.

It is intolerance, which makes you blind,
Secluded self-opinion, of any right.
Mangled in existence, to convey
Pessimism, pervade the light,
Miasma radiates her indecency,
And cries, 'I am a woman of proud mien!'

Freedom - Be Damned!

I can still taste your excitement.
Spartacus, I whisper,
Under my breath.
You know my tendency
To break regalia!

How tender the story, the lost moons,
My insight and abandon,
Every incited word.
Intention or demon,
Freedom - Be damned!

Perplex, the complex of love,
The laughter of the brigadiers.
Break the spell, I say out loud -
And then, out of harms way,
Swear, intensely.

Shadows

Civilisation, the hunter,
Preys upon the wasted shadows.
Dancing,
Are demons in his eyes?

I dare him not
To see me,
I dare him,
Kiss the resolute.

In all ages, beyond life,
Did time and again
Rise, from its own destruction,
Out of succession and demise.

I could not love him.
He flew, like a bird,
And I humbled myself with belief,
He knew, that I loved him.

I dream again,
Stallions, the wild lands,
How I shared the saddle,
A rider without territory.

Impetuous and salient, gilded
Like a modern aristocrat.
Jump at command!
I will arrange my necessity.

John Harrold

My name is John Harrold and I am 64 years old at present. I started writing poetry many years ago now, but never thought that it was good enough to pursue for publishing purposes.

I originate from London and now live in South Wales. In my time at work (in several jobs over the years), I have been to many places and have seen people, countryside, nature and other things as well, which have been inspirational in my poetry. But, the biggest inspiration for me has been my Christian faith and love for God which also comes out in a lot of my poems.

Of late some of my poems have made me start to think of my soon to come retirement from working as in the poem Tomorrow.

I like writing poems and short stories and so far I have had over fifty poems published and several articles as well.

I hope to be able to carry on writing after I retire and seeing more of my work in print so that I can bless others with the thoughts and ideas that come my way.

It was through the Triumph House team that I have gained the confidence to write more as they have published most of my work to date.

Another publisher put one of my poems fourth out over 1200 poems in a competition, but so far I have not won any prizes, but that does not mater so much as I like writing about life as I see it.

Here's to a lot more poems to be written (and hopefully a few prizes as well).

Forgive Us Lord

Lord, please break down the spirit
that has divided Your church.
Forgive us for the things that
we have said and have also done,
to divide Your holy people.

Lord, build up the right spirit
that will unite us together,
in our hearts and minds to
grow in love for Your people
and in our love just for You.

Choices

We all have choices
that we must make.
Adam blamed Eve,
she blamed the snake.

God said to Adam
to go and create.
Adam listened to Eve,
who listened to the snake.

We all have choices
that we must make.
But, if they are wrong,
don't blame the snake.

Leaves

See them flying in the wind,
see them flying high.
Big leaves, small leaves,
brown leaves, dead leaves,
blowing up the hill and down the lane.
They don't stay still long
as here comes the wind again.

On Hadrian's Wall

They came to build Hadrian a wall,
(boys and men all strong and tall)
from the Tyne to the Solway Firth.

Why build a wall so strong and stout?
'To keep those awful Scotsmen out,'
the soldiers of Rome would shout.

Still people come from far and wide
to stand and look with passion and pride,
at this wall, once so long and tall.

It seems that this wall will never fall
come weather, wind, snow, hail or rain,
this wall is going to forever remain.

Loneliness

In a quiet, lonely little church
in the front pew a lonely man sat.
Before him on a trestle table
a lonely box draped in black.
No mourners, no family, no friends
came to console him in his loss.
This had been his only friend.
She had been his whole life,
this was her lonely end,
she had been his loving wife.

An Ode To Teeth

Oh, good grief,
I'm losing my teeth.
Oh, how sad,
they all went bad.
Goodbye old friends,
the dentist now makes amends.
With choppers anew,
I'll eat roast beef and stew.
But, I'm sure going to miss you.
I expect you already knew,
when the dentist took a look
and noted in his little book
that the parting of the ways
was only in a few more days.
But, I will remember you
my teeth once so new.

Memories

Memories fade as we grow old
of summers hot, and winters cold,
and yet we think of times
when happiness like sunshine shines,
of weddings and birthdays.

Memories still fade as of old
we remember loved ones still and cold.
Those who have lived their earthly day
and now lie buried beneath the clay.
Ah, they were the sad, sad, sad days.

Memories come, and still they go,
they melt like the white winter snow,
and still we cherish the time
when we heard the clock strike nine,
when we were young and gay.

Memories are not what they used to be,
we recall only what we want to see,
and reject all that was bad or sad,
the things that did not make us glad,
oh, to think of what we used to be.

Tomorrow

Criticise me not, my son,
for growing old and full of sorrow.
Where I am today
you may be there tomorrow.

Where I was yesterday,
you are there today
but of tomorrow
who knows what might be?

So, criticise me not my son
for growing old and full of sorrow,
as you may not live
to see the new tomorrow.

This Is Our Land

From the lofty Scottish Highlands
to the lowliest of Glens.
From the high points of Wales
and the Eastern English Fens,
God's handiwork is found
all over this hallowed ground.
Visit the Dales and the Lakes,
and the shores of Erin too,
these show what God can do.
From county to county,
in every part of the land,
it is amazing to see
the work of a creator,
from a great Creator's hand.

The Sailor

Home is the sailor,
Home from the sea.
Home is the boy,
Home for his tea.
Home on the land
Small yacht in hand.
How far to the sea?
Just the boating lake
on the village pond
near to his home,
is where this sailor
spent his days at sea.

The Quietness Of Nature

You do not hear a snowflake fall,
or the tide turn in ebb and flow.
The clouds in the sky bump
without making a single sound.
Each morning rises the dew
up from the ground.
This is the silence of God
found only in the natural round.

The Life Of Some People

A wild foaming tide,
a raging roaring sea.
No sun to be seen,
and no star to guide.
This seems to be the life
that some people lead.
Being tossed to and fro
not knowing where to go.

Their lives are messed up
with drink, drugs and sex.
They live for the now,
and care not of tomorrow.
No wonder they are like
the wild raging, foaming tide.

They live without a guide
who could lead them safely
to a better way of life.
Only God can still the raging
that is hidden deep inside
of every tormented life.

Rejoice In God

I rejoice in God my saviour.
I rejoice in the love that you give.
I rejoice in your strength alone.
I am, and will have, nothing on my own.
I rejoice when you call me to dine,
At your lovely table, freshly spread.
I rejoice when you give me what I need.
The food for growth, on which I feed.
I rejoice in you, oh, I rejoice in you.
My God, my saviour and my friend.

I Am Blessed

(Written on the Mount of Beatitudes, Israel on 24.06.04)

Blessed is my mind
when I think His way.
Blessed is my mouth
in what I say.
Blessed are my ears
in what I hear.
Blessed are my hands
to do His work.
Blessed are my feet
in my daily walk.
Blessed is my heart
to sing His praise.
Blessed is my life
to serve in many ways.
All of this I find
is because I'm blessed in mind.

Memorial Stones

There they stand in neat rows,
giving name, rank and number,
of the men who died fighting
so that we could be free.

These stones cannot speak, but,
yet they can still remind us
of the men. Once an army.
These men used to call out
their name, rank and number
when at attention on parade.

But now they are all so silent
as they lie there in the grave.
They paid the price to set us free,
and to ride the world of tyranny.

Longings 09/02/2004

I long to hear Your voice
I long to see Your face
I long to worship You
When I come into this place.

I need to hear Your voice
I need to see Your face
I need to worship You
When I enter this holy place.

One day I shall hear Your voice
One day I shall see Your face
One day I shall worship You
In Your Heavenly place.

Just Me Getting Old

I am alright really,
but now I cannot see
since I had one glass eye
fitted into the left socket.

I am alright really
but now it's the teeth
as they are plastic ones
I find it very hard to eat.

I am alright really,
but now it is the knee
needing a new joint to
be just like the other one.

I am alright really
but now it is my hip that is
out of joint, and needs renewing
so that I can walk without a stick.

I am alright really,
as my strength nearly is gone.
So to cheer myself up,
I go and put the kettle on.

Jay Thomas

This is the world of dreams.

I had wandered the land, eyes to the ground, shackled by the constraints inherent in the human oddity. But when I raised my head, an exaltation of larks fractured the sky, snapping a fault line in my mind. A deluge of enlightenment rained down where reality and hope convene. Where vast dreamscapes open up, their boundaries confined only by the limits of our imagination.

My poetry comes from this place; where fact meets fiction, where aspirations become concrete. However, mostly within human endeavour there is a sinister underhand side. Our insecurities, our selfishness, greed, avarice, slip unnoticed into our dreamscapes, smothering, contaminating and stifling the space. Reeking like death. And then our worlds snap shut sending us ugly, insecure, still greedy back to the void.

The poems are often merely glimpses through these doors to another existence. Other times they describe the aftermath of an opening snapped shut. And other times the nightmare which our dreams and realities become.

'The intelligence sowed in us like a virus' - (to paraphrase R S Thomas) coupled with the painfully slow evolution of our base desires and instincts, ensures that our moments of enlightenment are short lived. And that dreams for some are nightmares for others, frequently as history shows us - with very real, frightening and fatal consequences. Our relationship with nature too, has moved beyond the boundaries of symbiosis, to a place where we are doing irreparable damage.

From a mythical fall from grace, an expulsion from the garden of Eden, a paradise lost, we search for enlightenment and inner peace. It is of our dreams for us and others, and our tenuous relationship with nature that the poems ask questions.

Quicksilver

The house was built with strong foundations,
concrete boarders raised with a firm hand
some years ago.
The floorboards in the front room
had to come up you know.
Hundreds of jerks with a claw hammer
and loud bends of old rusted nails through
woodworm infested timber.

Every last one came up.
Some were remembered.
We quenched our thirst throughout the day
and that night roasted seventy odd years
of dry sticks; sweet smelling birch stabbing
the clear full moon lit air.
Mesmerised by the glow
we slung the planks on the pyre
watching slowly as the shades in embers popped,
sending dark butterflies floating on the warm air.

The next day the sun beat down on the charred path
as I shovelled spent fuel from the hip over the fence.
Onto another dream.

Reflections

I imagine a life for this bird.
Easing through the low lying branches,
bobbing and weaving from song to song,
soaring and diving in words alone.
Two - a penny, priceless through the air

then blown to the grass to paint a masters tragedy.
I raise it from the ground and face the Styx;
my dreams reflecting in the water.
Melting like Icarus and on my descent.
Then it dropped; lifeless from my hands.

To soar again!
Whistling through my mind.

En Passant

We met on a ledge. A check discovered.
The pin had flow, the prize remained.
Awkward and jutting, looking once
it cracked gnawed bones on slate.

And I stared. Skewered. Simian amazed
at the night black rook bossing the
carrion cliffs; judging the
barren tundra. It glanced a

waiting move and cut the icy wind
with cackles at the thought of my
broken sticks hammered on the rocks.
Taking my eyes for breakfast.

One instinct sent me reeling on the anvil's
edge. I steadied myself.
Yet could still imagine how
good it would look on my bookcase.

Driving Fast

I would not have rallied
but for your perfume:
so right.
I glare down an old road.
We'll go there again.

It's all such a blur that
we end up driving fast,
away from us,
snatching the wheel -
spiralling down
through the air.

Clutching each other when
the impact never comes

Mad March

Time has moved us on
and an advent calendar
still sits on the geometric
fireplace.

Doors half closed.

I've a bottle of gin where
a bedside table should be.
There's a few glasses
your side.

Let's take time together.

I'll open the odd
numbers, you
have the even.

Sun Snakes

I had come so far
from the trees
to see sun snakes,
writhe peaceful
in the bright apple sun.

An orgy of colours
folding on the stones.
My hind legs rattling
the rocks; heaving
closer with heavy
headed momentum.

From cracks in reason
they come, sliding
beauty, whispering heat.
Licking the air with
precision.

Hot and cavorting,
they taste my
lazy wonderment.
Ready as ever to strike.

The Wine

You bought wine
and came flowing in,
all bubbly,
crimson cheeked
and merry.

Too much! I said.

You did not
deserve it
but that night I
had it anyway;
with hard cheese.

Some day it may
cost me everything.

April Fool

I must be a fool
to gaze at April
butterflies

waltzing along
the hedgerows.

As May and
June fluttered
admirably by,

my heart opened,
and life coursed
through my soul.

Enlightenment

There's a front blowing in.
A fierce mass of grey
charging the headland,
menacing a pallid sky.

Old maps, top sails
and dusty masts
adorn the shelves
beneath the keeper's gaze.

Treacherous gulls have
flown the battered
lighthouse fast.
Evading reason's storm.

The keeper swings his feet.
A storm engulfs the
silver land. A crown and
thirty tarnished pennies drop.

A Thought

The universe increases its space,
extends in time.
Until it expands into everything
it is ever going to be.

And then it expands into everything
it ever was.

Ice Wands

We picked out ice wands
from reeds dipping by a frozen brook.
In thick coats we cast spells
in the white wood
and decorated fields with messages;
listened with glee as streams
ground to whistling glass;
looking back at the magic as we slid
home.

We slept by the fireside 'till noon.
The sun beamed through the curtains
and we ran back through the woods -
quick as children. Reeds dripped to the
tune - full - flowing water,
the wood was glistening in the emerald light
and fields were green for miles.

I looked at you in awe.
And melted in your eyes like magic.

Belief

We talked about belief
and you cried its
shortcomings.
All faithless.
Fist against the rain
and back to the trees.
We were sorry.

Salvation

It started to rain hard that morn
roaring rivers like a bad dream.
Poor sods perishing on a bleak midwinter,
pale and slouched, carried on a raging storm.

Years of soot drifting on the breeze
hung nervous on a cyclone's lip.
Grey mists across a field of bones and ashes
shake the sombre dead

clothed and helpless in the rain,
demons clutching at their ankles.
The dispossessed scream in vain
like stray, black dogs barking for the Lord -

a crowd of voices in reverence of
Gods created in man's image.
In the end comes rain.
Slow but sure as winter.

The Word

Through the rain the black cloak comes
- daggers drawn
in the still of the mind.

In a dark yet glitzy dreamscape
heavily made up drunks
flirt with reality,

ambling through the corpses;
standing on the backs of the dead.

With temporal delusion
black ecclesiastic robes
cut out profane tongues.

But when the scholar's boat
sunk on the Styx
a mass of voices called to silence the howl.

Jason Whitehall

I started writing at the age of about 12. I was never really interested in school as I spent a lot of my time being chased by bullies with rocks and sticks. It wasn't until I found a book on an older friend's bookshelf by the Australian poet Nan Witcomb (The Thoughts of Nanuska), that I began to write. Her words inspired me and made me feel like I wasn't alone in the world.

Although you can see her influence in a couple of my poems I believe I have my own style and she was merely a catalyst to open me up to possibilities (thank you Nan) . . .

My poetry has many themes from woes of society and the heavy hand of establishment to the burdens and blessings of love. Some of my poetry can only be described as spiritual and enlightened. The funny thing is about these poems in particular is that when I write them I tend to go into a trance-like state. They are written very quickly and when I've finished writing them and re-read them, I am sometimes blown away by what I've written.

I really enjoy writing and for me it's almost like therapy, a kind of release. Often when I write I can be feeling quite down or angry. I don't really write for anyone but me, but I do like the idea of another person reading my poetry, perhaps being in the same place of mind that I was when I wrote it and getting comfort from the words in that they're not alone. If someone else in the world has experienced the same pain or loss or loneliness I hope to ease the pain of a lover's broken heart or to help let a lost adolescent feel a little more found or a lonely soul feel like he has a friend. I am happy with that . . .

It makes my heart smile to think I may help another person feel a little better with my words . . .

Adolescent Crisis

The natural inspirations
And imageries of youth,
Have been left *far* behind,
No longer baring its fruits . . .
Replaced by artificial cause,
Shrouded by shadows of falsified law . . .
Once my existence and all that I knew
Had a wholeness that humbled my soul,
Until I was burdened by a painful despair,
That clawed at my heart,
Taking terrible toll . . .
Forever this ill event tainted and marred,
All future access to my wondrous past,
Where all dreams we're granted,
Free of guilt, free of charge,
From an infinite well of passion so vast . . .
Ignorance ensured that the wounds in my heart,
Had sacrificed all hope of a fresh, brand new start . . .
The precious gifts that my birthright was blessed,
Could not handle the blows that my real life confessed . . .
Until I was blinded, an empty shell, merely led
By the elusions my brain was constantly fed . . .
Deceived by the tyranny of self abuse,
Injecting its lies, I make *no* refuse . . .
A poisonous mask, a pitiful excuse,
That rapes me of origin and hinders all truth . . .
Don't ask me why, for I cannot explain,
Why I gave up my dreams, so I wouldn't feel pain . . .
If given a chance to do it again,
I'd let my tears flow,
Like a river,
Like rain . . .
For the chance to imagine,
To inspire the flame,
That fuels the sweet blessings,
Of pleasure and pain . . .

Astral Waltz

The sun kisses my naked flesh
And I am warm to my core.
It satisfies my every wish,
From where I don't know,
It opens a door.
It releases my inner sanctum, my mind is alive
As the warmth spreads on, refreshes, renews,
As a new day has dawned.
The kisses once timid are now more insistent.
A calm intensity remains me how persistent,
My mind, like the sun, strips me bare.
Unprotected from the exquisite unknown energy.
Mind and body craving shade and sanctuary.
A place to rest in eternal harmonic balance.
In perfect unison, the sun takes the moon in
Hand and ushers her toward the evening waltz.
Garish Light Retreat, Ends this dance.

Angelic Monsters

The outer perception had eyes of an angel,
the inner was beastly and cruel.
My heart was aflow with the lyrics of love,
my mind was replying, 'You fool.'
The delicate fingers that played with my soul,
had nails as sharp as a knife.
Twas for grasping my love I thought to conceal,
they were really for taking my life.
Since then I've discovered love isn't through sight,
it's what rests in the inner that counts.
For the outside is there to bait the next catch
and the inner for catchers to doubt.

Angels In Disguise

Sometimes the best advice
that can be given,
does not come from friends,
family nor lovers.

It often comes from mysterious strangers,
alluring passers-by
that seem to fly out of your life,
as swiftly as they flew into it.

Leaving behind them
a pocketful of hope
and the seeds of inspiration.

Maybe the reason they seem to fly
in and out of your life so swiftly,
is because they are really,
angels in disguise.

Cupid's Delight

We're here to love,
our hearts to fill.
To will, to will,
thy gracious will.
To give up thyself,
unto another,
forever connected,
to thy lover.
Joined by silver thread of light,
a path for two, to one, unite.
Unveils the journey of Cupid's flight
and reveals the gifts of pure delight.
So learn to love,
your hearts do fill
and will, to will,
thy gracious will.

Flight Of Delight

Follow me down roads unknown,
Trust my heart you're not alone,
Take my hand into the night,
For all that comes to mind,
Behold now cometh all alight,
For you and I as one,
Shall be the strength,
As if to carry on all great might, that one,
Shall grasp for eternity throughout all the night . . .
With great eternal wings of light,
To fly off softly through this night,
In gracious and harmonious flight,
Becomes our union and delight,
Now for once and evermore,
Shall thy wings of freedom soar,
Be able to fly from all denial, criticism, hate and all that sigh . . .
Releasing our souls from the tackles of hate,
Unleashing a new and refreshing fate,
Allowing these wings of freedom to soar,
Shows the life that we led,
Is our choice to ignore . . .

Just Out Of Time

A figure of loveliness, mother nature's design,
Not out of compassion, just out of time.
A statue of manhood, the peak of his prime,
Not out of desire, just out of time.
A child of the earth, not yet found reason nor rhyme,
Not out of love, just out of time.
A chance in a womb, before the month reaches nine,
Not out of spirit, just out of time.
A misplaced youth that found the needle sublime,
Not out of hope, just out of time.
A bag of bad blood, it's hard to define,
Not out of luck, just out of time.

Love Is Told . . .

Love tears, love scares
The fertile mares that dare to care,
The fragile hearts with barbed-wired snares.
A revolving fair, a lonely lair,
A precious gift, a dream so rare,
Love tears, love scares . . .

Love is bold, love is told,
Through naive eyes, not yet turned cold,
And nubile moulds, waiting to be sold,
Will soon be rolled under harsh hands fold,
For someone old to keep and hold . . .

Love is cold, love is bold,
Love is sold and love is told,
Love will always be told . . .

No . . . On

No hope, no dreams,
No luck, no faith,
No love, no mates,
No money, no grace,
No sex, no lust,
No peace, no drugs,
No rush, no mind,
No fun, no time!

On hope, on dreams,
On luck, on faith,
On love, on mates,
On money, on grace,
On sex, on lust,
On peace, on drugs,
On rush, on mind,
One fun, on time!

Ode To Love

I tried to write a poem today of love and all its glory,
And I decided that this concept was a more than familiar story.
Of how you want their touch, when you can't have it,
Or how they want your touch, when you don't want it.
I could talk about the hurt and throbbing pain that plagues
Your heart, or the emptiness that takes control when lovers are apart.
Or how about the feelings that you get when they are near,
You forget about bad feelings, like hate and pain and fear . . .
It's hard to place these feelings, if you have loved, you'd know,
Like me, that their love is purely yours to keep, and your heart
Returns these special feelings, freely unto thee.
As if it were a second nature, a past known language of the heart,
That spreads throughout your very being, when Cupid's arrow,
First makes its mark.
Yes love will always blossom and sometimes it may break,
But we travel onwards, living, learning, giving what it takes . . .

Perpetual Circles Of Wisdom

People search and people strive,
To find a meaning to their lives . . .

They travel the globe and attempt to acquire,
Their hopes, their dreams, their heart's desire . . .

They find pieces of puzzles and put them together,
But to find all the pieces could take them forever . . .

Some keep to their quest and the whole world they roam,
Whilst some find the answers, all along were at home . . .

When the wisdom they gathered, let them realise,
That the meaning they wanted, was in front of their eyes . . .

The perpetual circles that they leave behind,
Is part of a journey to find their divine . . .

So if you hear a calling that tells you to go,
There's only one thing that I want you to know . . .

Though you may gain wisdom
The things you adore,
May sometimes be found
Outside your front door.

Prisoners Of Love

Pity not the pallid heart,
Bestow no sympathy,
Fuel not the hungry fires of want,
Donate no empathy.
Revoke the understanding touch,
And counteract all care.
Dub compassion null and void,
And leave all mercy bare.
A poisoned mind of broken dreams,
That's bitter to the taste.
Becomes a safety blanket,
That disguises all true face.
A demented scar of pain and angst,
That tortures and demeans
A blinded love that lives a lie
In too many a victim's dreams.

Slipstream

When two souls meet they have the capacity
To exchange the infinite
Wisdom's of the ages
And release the cosmic energies
That open up the cages
Of the birds that sing the songs of pace
That harmonise the air
And
Allow the bright sensations
Of tenderness to flare.
So slipstream thus
Did take these souls
On a ride on life's fluid wings
With all the joy and happiness
That cosmic contact brings.
A ride designed to take these souls
A costume made carriage
For spirits alike
For union of two
For two to unite
Moulds two into one
As it flies through the night.

Spotlight Poets Information

We hope you have enjoyed reading this book - and that you will continue to enjoy it in the coming years.

If you are interested in becoming a Spotlight Poet then drop us a line, or give us a call, and we'll send you a free information pack.

Alternatively if you would like to order further copies of this book or any of our other titles, then please give us a call or visit our website at www.forwardpress.co.uk

Spotlight *Poets*

Spotlight Poets Information
Remus House
Coltsfoot Drive
Peterborough
PE2 9JX

Telephone: 01733 898102

Email: spotlightpoets@forwardpress.co.uk